Trails
with
Tales

Trails with Tales

intriguing walks around
LEIGHTON MOSS, SILVERDALE & ARNSIDE

BETH & STEVE PIPE

First published in 2017
by Palatine Books,
Carnegie House,
Chatsworth Road
Lancaster LA1 4SL
www.palatinebooks.com

British Library Cataloguing-in-Publication data
A catalogue record for this book is available from the British Library

Paperback ISBN 13: 978-1-910837-08-5

Designed and typeset by Carnegie Book Production
www.carnegiebookproduction.com

Printed and bound by Multiprint

*This book is dedicated to the many cakes
of Leighton Moss, without which none of
this would have been possible.*

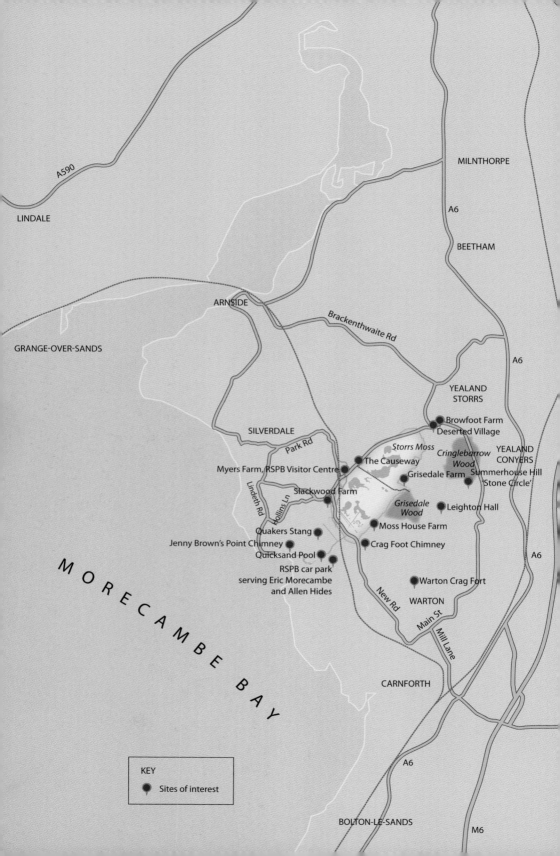

A590

LINDALE

MILNTHORPE

A6

BEETHAM

ARNSIDE

Brackenthwaite Rd

GRANGE-OVER-SANDS

YEALAND
STORRS

Browfoot Farm
Deserted Village

SILVERDALE

Storrs Moss

Cringlebarrow Wood

YEALAND
CONYERS

Park Rd

The Causeway

Myers Farm, RSPB Visitor Centre

Grisedale Farm

Summerhouse Hill
'Stone Circle'

Slackwood Farm

Grisedale Wood

Leighton Hall

Lindeth Rd

Hollins Ln

Quakers Stang

Moss House Farm

Jenny Brown's Point Chimney

Quicksand Pool

Crag Foot Chimney

RSPB car park
serving Eric Morecambe
and Allen Hides

Warton Crag Fort

New Rd

WARTON

A6

Main St

Mill Lane

M O R E C A M B E   B A Y

CARNFORTH

KEY

Sites of interest

BOLTON-LE-SANDS

M6

Acknowledgements

OUR FIRST and biggest debt of thanks goes to Andy Denwood for his wonderful history of the area, *Leighton Moss: Ice Age to Present Day*, which inspired us to create this series of walks enabling everyone to visit the sites he describes, plus a few others besides.

Thanks also to the Mourholme Local History Society for the detailed and painstaking research they undertake, separating out fact from fiction, and enabling us to better understand how the area came to be the way we see it today.

Additional thanks go to everyone at the RSPB Leighton Moss, who have humoured us, allowed us to borrow items for photos and supported us as we tackled this project, and also to Morecambe Bay Partnership for the loan of books and for running workshops and events that have helped us to uncover more of the mysteries that surround the bay.

Nothing in this book would have been possible if Palatine Books hadn't kindly agreed to work with us and we are hugely indebted to Lucy, Anna and the rest of the team for taking our words and pictures and transforming them into the beautiful book you now see before you. Thank you. A million times, thank you – we definitely owe you cake!

Final thanks to Arnside and Silverdale AONB who do such a magnificent job with their team of volunteers, all working hard to keep the entire area in tip top condition – for us and for the wildlife.

Introduction

LEIGHTON MOSS and the surrounding area will always have a special place in our hearts. Back in 2011 we took the huge and life changing decision to leave our life in Hampshire and relocate to the region where Steve grew up. We risked everything and spent the first three months of 2011 living in our campervan in Silverdale while we desperately hunted for a house.

Funds were low and walks are cheap so we spent a lot of time exploring the area, discovering tracks and trails that, judging by how overgrown they were, weren't being walked by many others.

The walks in here are some of the routes we explored back then, woven around new routes to tie in as many of the elements of Andy Denwood's book as possible. You may find some tracks a little overgrown and, therefore, some of the waymarkers a little bit hidden, but for us that's part of the charm; knowing you're exploring somewhere that's a little bit off the usual beaten track.

Other routes visit the 'can't miss' hot spots with jaw dropping views and fascinating folklore, but so far as we can we've shared a little of our local knowledge to help you explore the area and, hopefully, fall in love with it as much as we have.

We've done our level best to be as accurate as we can with the directions but it's not always possible to describe a route in a way that 100% of people will agree with. We've bickered our way around all of the routes several times, arguing the toss about 'slight left' versus 'half left' and whether or not we need to mention another flipping kissing gate. We've tried really hard, but if you spot something that's not quite right, please do let us know. We've also provided an 'escape route' for most walks just in case you prefer something a little shorter.

Each of the routes mentions the distance to the nearest railway stations but we've excluded bus routes, mainly because they tend to change often and without warning, whereas we figure that neither Arnside nor Silverdale stations are going anywhere for a while. There are a number of local bus routes so just check the internet for Arnside and Silverdale buses to find the latest timetables and routes.

We're fortunate enough to be able to spend plenty of time walking, bird watching and sampling the fantastic array of cakes in the visitors' centre at Leighton Moss so, if you see us, pop over and say hello and we'll maybe let you in on some other secret spots to visit too.

Beth writes the words, Steve takes all the lovely photos and if you want to see more of either or both, take a look at our blog: www.cumbrianrambler.blogspot.co.uk where you can follow more of our adventures.

Contents

Fairy Steps

WALK 1

Sandside–Fairy Steps

Start:	Seafront at Sandside
Grid Ref:	SD 47399 80532
Distance:	8 km / 5 miles
Terrain:	Hard track, forest track, tarmac. A mainly woodland walk with some very short sections along the road.
Parking:	Free car parking at Sandside
Public Transport:	Arnside train station 3.2 km (2 miles) from the start of the walk
Facilities:	No facilities along the route.
Note:	Please check tide times and levels prior to beginning this route as Sandside is prone to flooding during particularly high tides.

Overview

This walk explores paths missed by many of the locals and follows ancient trails in use since man first visited the area. There's some fascinating geology to spot in the outcrops along the railway cutting and some interesting folklore around the ancient fairy steps – will you be able to get to the top without touching the sides?

View from Arnside Knott

Route

Keeping the estuary on your right, walk along the footpath and then continue on the road as it starts to rise towards the bridge. Take the path to the left leading down to the disused railway line (look for the Beetham Parish Information Board), then turn left to walk along the railway cutting.

At the far end pass through a kissing gate and bear right then left along a lane. Continue on for 50 m until you see the way marked sign for Yans Lane. Follow the path up into the woods – immediately before the large parking bay turn right up the woodland path and right out onto the track again at the top.

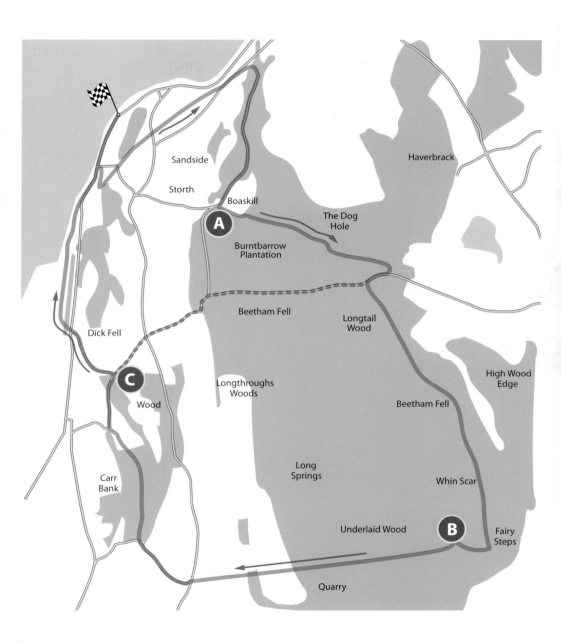

Sandside

Storth

Boaskill

A

Haverbrack

The Dog
Hole

Burntbarrow
Plantation

Beetham Fell

Longtail
Wood

Dick Fell

C

Wood

Longthroughs
Woods

High Wood
Edge

Beetham Fell

Carr
Bank

Long
Springs

Whin Scar

Underlaid Wood

B

Fairy
Steps

Quarry

Sandside cutting

Keep right at the fork and continue on until you reach a hard track – turn right here towards the houses. Opposite the large white house turn left to cross a stone stile signed 'Haverbrack Bank and Cockshot Lane'. (**Point A**) Remain on this path following the waymarkers over the next stone stile and up through the woodland. When you reach a T junction turn right and continue down to the road.

Turn right along the road and after 50 m cross the stone stile on the left signed 'Slackhead and Hazel Slack'.

[*Exit point for short walk: continue on along the road to* **Point C**.]

Follow this broad track till you reach a stone cairn with a plaque pointing the way to the Fairy Steps. Bear ahead and right to follow this path then keep to the main path – don't go down the path to the gate signed as 'Game wildlife area'. Continue on through the coppiced woodland till you reach a signed path junction and take the turning left to Fairy Steps. (**Point B**)

Climb up the Fairy Steps to the viewpoint then either return to the foot of the Fairy Steps via the steps or via the clearly marked detour. Return back to the signed path junction and this time follow the route down to Hazelslack. Continue on down through another limestone cutting and through the woodland and fields until you reach the road.

Take the road opposite leading down past Hazelslack Tower and continue on until you reach Teddy Heights AONB woodland on the right – follow the path through the woodland signposted to Storth.

At the end of the woods pass through the kissing gate and continue on until you reach the road. Turn right to follow it uphill then turn left into Guard Hill Lane (**Point C**) and follow it down to the main road.

Cross the road with care and turn right to reach a gate a few yards up. Pass through the gate and out onto the old railway embankment along the estuary. Turn right and follow the embankment back to starting point at Sandside.

A tale about fairies, folklore and freight trains

The first section of this route follows a wonderful hidden gem; the Sandside cutting. There are people who've lived in the area for years and not found this secluded little footpath. It follows part of the route of the old Arnside to Hincaster branch line – you can trace the old branch line on an OS map as it runs from the viaduct at Arnside to Hincaster just south of Kendal (which is well worth a visit if you're in the area for a while).

The branch line opened in 1876 and moved coal and iron ore from County Durham across to the ironworks at Barrow-in-Furness, avoiding the busy junction at Carnforth. It also carried passengers between Kendal and Grange-over-Sands – a route that was known locally as the Kendal Tommy. Due to its role in moving munitions around during World War One it was known as the 'Lifeline of Britain'. The passenger route ended in 1942 with much of the tracks being removed in the 1960s – but a short stub from Sandside to Arnside continued to operate through until 1972 moving limestone from the local quarries.

If you've ever wondered what a coppiced woodland looks like then the stretch of the route leading up to the Fairy Steps will show you. The area is full of hazel trees (giving Hazelslack its name – slack coming from the old English word for gully or ravine) and the unmistakable clusters of straight stems shooting up from one base is particularly noticeable during the winter months when the trees are bare.

Sandside cutting

Coppiced trees

The Fairy Steps themselves are surrounded in mystery, myth and folklore. There are various versions of the story but the most common one is that if you can climb to the top of the steps without touching the sides a fairy will grant you a wish (for many of us that wish may simply be to sit down, catch our breath and enjoy the view!).

The Fairy Steps marked an important junction in the local ancient pathways – the paths from Storth and Arnside converged here on their way to the shop in Beetham. There used to be an iron ring in the rock near the top of Fairy Steps which was used for threading ropes and lowering parcels of flour, grain etc. on the return journey.

Fairy Steps

The route from the Fairy Steps down to Hazelslack is also a well known coffin route, though it must have been interesting navigating the Fairy Steps. Down in the farm adjacent to Hazelslack Tower there's a room with no windows where coffins were stored during the winter months when it was too risky to move them.

The road running past Hazelslack Tower is another old route but it served a very different purpose – it was used during the eighteenth century to move iron ore from the old pier at Sandy Bank across to the furnace at Leighton Beck (see Walk 7).

Hazelslack Tower was traditionally thought to have been one of a series of three towers (the others being Dallam and Arnside) built during the fifteenth century for the three daughters of a wealthy local landowner. This is now largely discredited and it's much more likely that they were built to provide protection from the Scottish raids. Hazelslack Tower was never fully completed and it was in ruins by 1811 – as you'll see from the walk it now forms part of a local farm and is very pretty in the spring when the cherry blossoms are out in the nearby orchard.

Hazelslack Tower

Old railway embankment

The estuary stretch of the walk is perfect for catching up on the local bird life with many interesting migrants stopping off during the year to swell the local native populations. The 'usual suspects' are all there – lapwings, oyster catchers, curlews, red shanks, ringed plovers and little egrets. These are joined through the year by assorted flocks of geese in the estuary and occasionally by clouds of waxwings descending on the local yew trees during the autumn – you may even be lucky enough to catch sight of avocets, mergansers and goosanders along the shoreline.

When you're on the shore near Sandside you might also want to keep your eyes peeled during the summer months for the local fishermen – not the rows of gentlemen with their fishing lines (always in residence during the incoming tide) but our local osprey family. They nest at Foulshaw Moss on the opposite side of the estuary and are often seen out hunting for fish at Sandside – for the past few years they've successfully fledged chicks and are particularly busy during June and July finding food to feed their rapidly growing brood.

Arnside Pier sunset

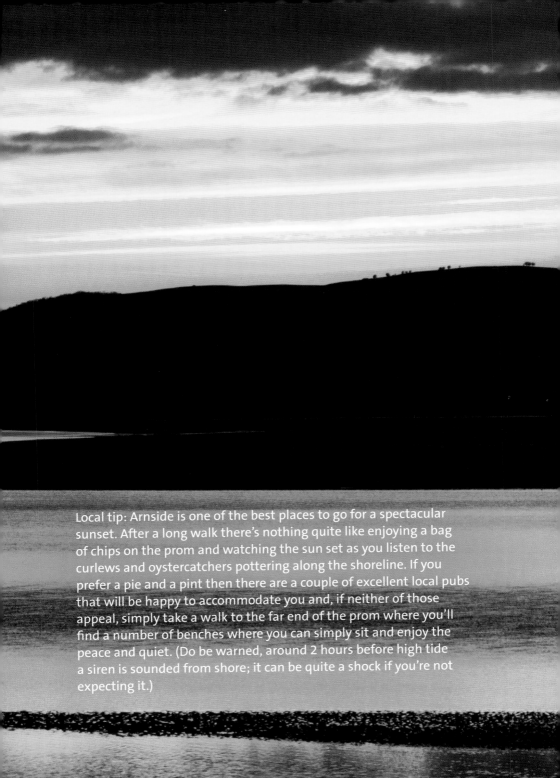

Local tip: Arnside is one of the best places to go for a spectacular sunset. After a long walk there's nothing quite like enjoying a bag of chips on the prom and watching the sun set as you listen to the curlews and oystercatchers pottering along the shoreline. If you prefer a pie and a pint then there are a couple of excellent local pubs that will be happy to accommodate you and, if neither of those appeal, simply take a walk to the far end of the prom where you'll find a number of benches where you can simply sit and enjoy the peace and quiet. (Do be warned, around 2 hours before high tide a siren is sounded from shore; it can be quite a shock if you're not expecting it.)

WALK 2

Arnside Knott

Start:	Silverdale Road lay-by near to Arnside Woods
Grid Ref:	SD 45862 77305
Distance:	6.5 km / 4 miles
Terrain:	Hard track, forest path, sand. This is a walk with options – at high tide stick to the woodland path around the coast and at low tide take a walk along the sand but please do NOT wander out into the bay – it may look inviting but it's incredibly dangerous.
Parking:	Free car parking in lay-by
Public Transport:	Arnside station (a 15 min walk if you start the route at New Barns)
Facilities:	Café at New Barns

Overview

The view from the top of Arnside Knott is possibly one of the finest views in the area. To the north are the Lakeland Fells, immediately beneath you the Kent Estuary sweeps through the landscape and away to your left Morecambe Bay opens up with its huge skies and ever-changing landscape.

Arnside Knott viewpoint

Route

From the lay-by cross the road then pass through the small wooden gate. Bear left following the path past the National Trust sign and in front of the limestone rock-face. Keep right at two small forks and remain on this path as it climbs gently and diagonally uphill and into the woodland.

When you reach a crossroads at a broad gravel track, turn left to swing down and around to a large wooden gate. Go through the gate and turn right along the path. When you reach a major path intersection go through the first gate then turn left and immediately through another gate. (**Point A**)

[*Exit point for short walk: turn right to follow path to benches at* **Point C**.]

Once through this gate continue for 20 m then take the right fork, climbing diagonally into the woods.

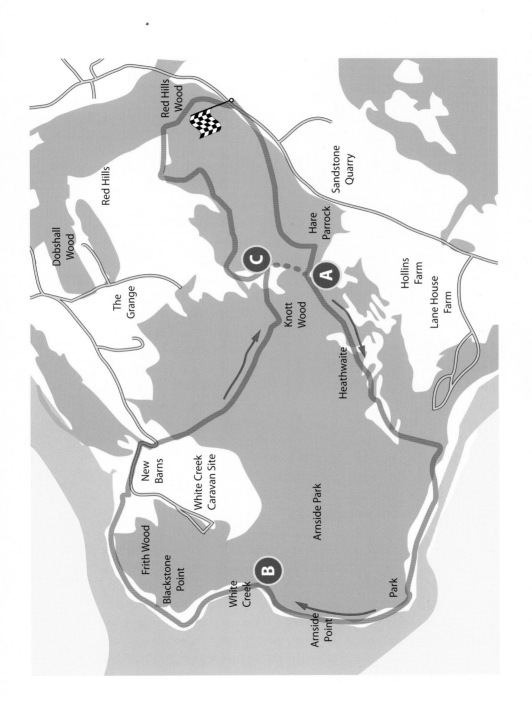

Remain on this path though the woods and out into open pasture (there's a nice diversion to your left here for gorgeous views down over Silverdale Cove). Continue along the main path until you reach another area of pasture, bear slight right (NOT hard right) to follow the path as it crosses the field ahead and drops down through woodland. (This is a pretty sharp descent but there are plenty of trees to hang on to). Keep going down through the woodland until you reach the broad flat track at the bottom.

Turn right along the track, through a large gap in a wall and then fork left, downhill, towards the coastline. Remain on the coastal path, running alongside the cliff edge until you reach a caravan site. Bear left towards two large wooden benches then turn left to emerge onto a large shingle beach. Turn right to walk along the back of the beach to the woodland on the far side and back up onto the coastal path. (**Point B**)

When the coastal path reaches a tarmac road follow the road along the back of the small bay and continue on it as it climbs around two sharp bends. At the second bend look for the enclosed path to the right signposted towards Arnside Knott. Continue ahead on this path, passing through a wooden gate, until you reach a wall. Turn left to follow the path alongside the wall to another gate. Pass through this gate and bear half left to follow a narrow gravel path as it climbs sharply up the hillside.

At the top of the path keep left in front of two benches (**Point C**) to reach a small gate. Once through the gate turn sharp right and follow the small path as it zigzags up the hill and leads out towards Arnside Knott viewpoint. From the view point turn right to follow a broad path into the woods and continue on as it joins a main track passing a distinctive 'h' shaped tree. When you see a large bench with panoramic views of the estuary, fork right to follow the smaller path leading through the woodland to the trig point.

Turn left at the trig point to drop down through the woods and rejoin the main track. Bear right then, after a few yards, left to go through a small wooden gate. Pass through the gate and turn right to follow the slightly smaller track down the broad hillside. At the bottom of the hill turn right and pass through another small gate in the wall, following the path signed initially to 'Arnside Tower' and then to 'Silverdale Road'.

When the path forks in front of a large yew tree, bear right to follow the path back to the starting point next to the large wooden gate.

h-shaped tree

Snowy fells

Silverdale Cove

A tale about huge hairy snakes and big bridges

There's so much to say about Arnside that it's hard to know where to start. Do we begin with the immense views, the heavy industry, the crashing bores or the flying serpents? To put your mind at rest we should probably begin with the serpents.

You'll be glad to know that the route doesn't pass directly through Haggs Wood where these stories originate but you can go and visit the woods (if you dare) as they are just a short walk from the lay-by at the start point. According to legend the 'Hagg Worms', or serpents, were huge, hairy and large enough to swallow birds. One story tells of a young boy who swears he saw a serpent fly up into a tree – he raced home in a state of terror to tell his story and the locals returned to burn the tree to the ground.

While I'm not one to doubt the word of an honest young man, and it's quite possible that reptiles exist in and around Haggs Wood, I'm not convinced they're huge, hairy and capable of flying – or at least if there are, you're much more likely to spot one on your way back from the pub than you are on your way there...

Silverdale Sands

Historically Arnside was a town of great importance, being the main starting out point for trips across the treacherous sands of Morecambe Bay. The sands may look golden and enticing at low tide on a sunny day but do resist the urge to stray from the shore on the coastal section of this walk. On one sunny bank holiday weekend in 2014 the fantastic team at Bay Search and Rescue (BSAR) were called to rescue a total of 28 people over the course of just three days.

As well as an important transportation point the town was also a busy fishery, though there have been many legal wrangles over the years concerning the fishing rights in the bay. Flat fish known as 'flooks' were the most common catch (giving rise to the town name of Flookburgh on the far side of the bay) and of course the bay has long been associated with cockling and shrimping.

During the nineteenth century when the port was at its height it was the import and export business that dominated the town, with the chief export being gunpowder from nearby Sedgwick. The main import was iron ore for the furnace at Leighton Beck (see Walk 7) which was bought in from Barrow across the bay.

Kent Estuary

Viaduct

The pier in the middle of Arnside is not original and was built by the railway company when they constructed the viaduct. It fell into disrepair but was saved and preserved thanks to the Morecambe Bay and Kents Bank Estuary Preservation Society. They had originally been formed to fight a plan from Manchester to dam and drain the bay – thankfully that plan fell through and instead they turned their attention to buying, protecting and restoring the pier.

The arrival of the railways in 1857 sounded the death knell for the shipping industry. Boats could no longer navigate up the river and although ships continued to dock at Blackstone Point (along the coastal section of the walk) it proved too difficult to transport the cargo over the marshes so it was eventually abandoned.

The viaduct crosses the estuary at an old fording point and was the first to be built using water jets in the construction of the supports. It was rebuilt and strengthened in 1915 to enable it to take the extra weight on the munitions trains from Barrow and last underwent a major refurbishment in 2011.

There had originally been plans to make the Arnside end of the viaduct into a sort of swing bridge to allow the passage of ships – this never happened but it does explain why the supports along this section are further apart. It wasn't the most ambitious railway plan in the area though; George Stephenson initially proposed a bridge running from Morecambe and stretching all the way across the bay to Ulverston on the far side. Sadly the scheme was considered too bold to attract enough backers so the viaduct was built instead.

Arnside is also home to one of the few regular tidal bores that can be seen around the UK and although the wave isn't high, it stretches the width of the bay and pretty much brings in the tide in one go. To catch the bore check the tide tables and look for a tide of over 9.5 m then head down to the pier an hour or two before high tide (it's not an exact science). You'll also be able to spot canoeists who like to ride the bore around the 'swing bridge' end of the viaduct, making good use of the wider spaced supports. Perhaps not the shipping use they originally had in mind when they built it, but being put to good use nevertheless.

Whitbarrow Scar

Causeway walker

WALK 3

Leighton Hall

Start:	RSPB Leighton Moss Visitors' car park
Grid Ref:	SD 47642 75050
Distance:	8 km / 5 miles
Terrain:	Tarmac, hard track, fields, forest track. A varied walk with some road walking at the start. Gentle ascents and one sharp descent through woodland
Parking:	Free car parking at Leighton Moss car park
Public Transport:	Silverdale train station 3 minutes' walk from start
Facilities:	Café and toilets in Leighton Moss visitors' centre

Overview

Our favourite thing about this route is the chance to see Leighton Moss from a different angle. The views from the field at the start of the walk are a great excuse to pause and catch your breath. Later in the walk the benches above Leighton Hall are the perfect spot to rest and enjoy your packed lunch as you take in the views of the hall, the moss and Morecambe Bay beyond.

Leighton Moss across to South Cumbria

Walk route

From Leighton Moss car park, return to the road and turn right, walking uphill and crossing the railway line. Turn left here and walk along the road and take the first turning on the left (towards Warton). There is no pavement in places so do take care.

Pass Slackwood Farm on your right and continue on, over the level crossing, until you reach Moss House Farm. Take the broad track to the left of the farm signed 'Coach Road', follow the track around to right and as it climbs and reaches the woodland, turn left onto a narrow signed route through the woods. (**Point A**)

When you reach another broad track, turn left to cross a gated stile, then continue up and across the field with excellent views of Leighton Moss below. Remain on the track as it curves round to the right and up through another gate, then continue on uphill, bearing left at the fork to pass through another gate.

Path through Leighton Park Woods

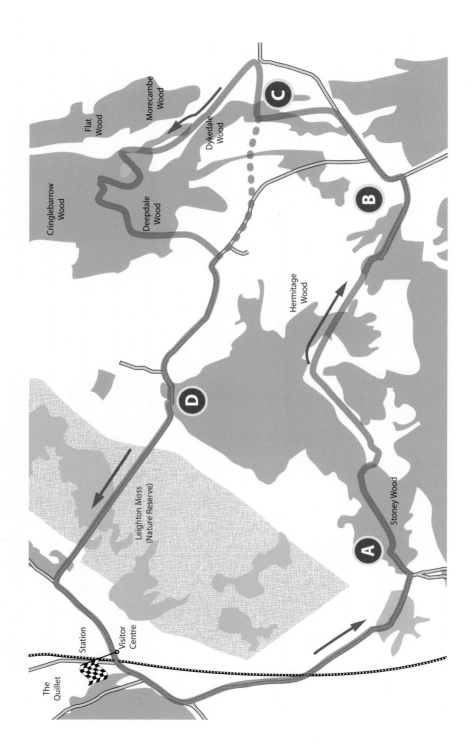

The Quillet

Station

Visitor Centre

Leighton Moss
(Nature Reserve)

Cringlebarrow
Wood

Flat
Wood

Morecambe
Wood

Deepdale
Wood

Dykedale
Wood

Hermitage
Wood

Stoney Wood

C

B

D

A

cricket being played on the flat grassy area to the front. The reason it is so elevated is apparently because when it was originally built the owner asked for it to be raised on a plinth of limestone blocks so he could see the ships docked in

Possible stone circle

Lancaster – there must have been far fewer trees back then for that to have been possible.

In the field around the summer house are the remains of, what some believe to be, a Bronze Age stone circle. The large boulders stand out on the broad level field and in 1935 a local archaeologist demonstrated that four of them lay along the circumference of a circle 140 metres across. There's no hard archaeological evidence for this other than that fact the boulders lie in apparent circular formation so it's entirely possibly they were simply left there by a retreating glacier – in fact recent geophysical surveys have shown no additional evidence whatsoever for the stone circle.

On the subject of things retreating – as you pass around Deepdale Pond you may be forgiven for expecting to find a body of water there. Old guidebooks describe it as a beautiful and picturesque glade and it remained a popular picnic spot up until the First World War. It's thought that an explosion at a munitions factory in nearby Lancaster in 1917 caused a fissure to open in the limestone and most of the water drained away leaving a geologically interesting, but rather less aesthetically pleasing, boggy marsh.

Rainbow over Leighton Moss

Burton Well

WALK 4

Leighton wells

Start:	RSPB Leighton Moss Visitors' car park
Grid Ref:	SD 47642 75050
Distance:	5.5 km / 3.5 miles
Terrain:	Tarmac, hard track, fields, forest track. A winding walk taking in a number of terrains. A couple of gentle ascents and one sharp descent down to Morecambe Bay
Parking:	Free car parking at Leighton Moss car park
Public Transport:	Silverdale train station 3 minutes' walk from start
Facilities:	Café and toilets in Leighton Moss visitors' centre

Overview

This really does feel like a secret walk as you wind your way through the woodlands around Silverdale discovering the ancient wells. Some are overgrown, others have been capped with pipes, but all of them tell a part of the story of the how the village came to be.

Lamberts Meadow bridge

Route

From the car park at Leighton Moss return to the road and turn right, walking uphill and crossing the railway line. Turn right walking along the road and just past the station until you see a waymarked path on your left crossing the golf course signed to Silverdale Village.

Follow the marked path across the golf course then pass through the kissing gate and turn right to follow the lane. Watch for the sign on your right showing the route to Dogslack Well – follow the track for approximately 100 m to visit the well then return to the road and continue the short distance along the road to Bank Well Pond. **(Point A)**

Turn left next to the information board and follow the path round the back of the pond then bear right as it rises to join another path. Continue down a flight of stone steps to reach the National Trust site at Lambert's Meadow.

Cross the meadow and the small wooden footbridge then turn left before the gate to follow the path to another gate at the end of the meadow. Pass through the kissing gate, with Burton Well on your left, and remain on the track until you reach the tarmac lane. Turn left here and continue on to the road.

At the road turn right, signposted to Silverdale, taking care as there are no pavements. Walk along the road for a short distance until you see a path on the left, signed Woodwell (immediately prior to The Chase). Don't cross into Pointer Woods but instead follow the enclosed track leading right alongside the woods to a stile. Cross the stile and follow the path as it runs between field and wall. At the end of the track turn left towards Woodwell and down to a kissing gate. **(Point B)**

Lamberts Meadow

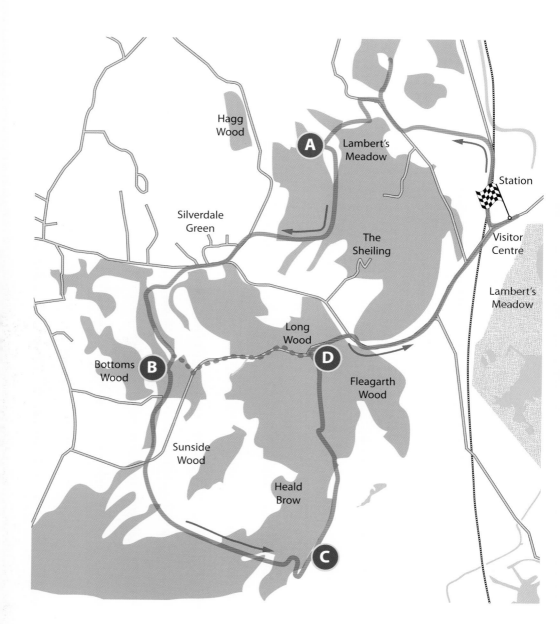

Hagg
Wood

A

Lambert's
Meadow

Station

Silverdale
Green

The
Sheiling

Visitor
Centre

Lambert's
Meadow

Long
Wood

D

Bottoms
Wood

B

Fleagarth
Wood

Sunside
Wood

Heald
Brow

C

[Exit point for short walk: walk straight across the field to the road, turn left and walk down the road to **Point D**.*]*

Take the path bearing right, down a small hill, towards Woodwell then follow it as it bends left to a gate and into the woods. Continue on along the cliff path, passing Woodwell below, until you reach the road. (*At this point you can, if you wish, follow the path bearing hard right downhill to take a closer look at Woodwell before returning to the route.*)

Cross the road and take path signed to Heald Brow and Quaker Stang. Continue to the end of the enclosed path, then left through a small woodland and out into open fields. Keep to the right hand field boundary as the path crosses two fields and descends steeply through woodland towards Morecambe Bay.

Once you reach the shoreline turn left (**Point C**), signposted to Fleagarth Wood and Hollins Lane, and follow the undulating path through the woodland until you reach the road (**Point D**). Turn right here, then right again and remain on this road until you reach the bridge across the railway. Turn right here to return to the car park.

A watery tale

We take running water for granted these days but the wells scattered around Silverdale give us a valuable insight into what life might have been like before mains water arrived, which happened a lot later than you probably think. The only true 'well' along this walk is Dogslack Well (which used to serve the houses in The Row) – and by that we mean the only typical underground, probably once dropped a bucket down to it 'Jack and Jill' type well – all of the others are springs and ponds, some natural and some that have clearly had a helping hand in shaping their function.

The springs appear thanks to the geology – limestone is a porous rock meaning water will happily permeate down through it until it meets an impervious layer, at which point the water will follow the route of the contact between to two rocks and appear at the surface as a spring. In this area there's a band of clay sitting underneath the limestone, forcing the water to the surface, and it's this action that has created the pond at Bank Well (it used to be a spring but has since formed into a pond). You can also see this process in action if you take a look under the cliff at Woodwell where the water continues to drip through into a hollowed-out animal trough.

Bank Well Pond

Initially the water would have been used mainly for human consumption but, as you can see by looking at the structures built around the wells, some were adapted for washing or providing water for farm stock. The large structure at Burton Well indicates its importance in serving the people of Silverdale Green, though they would have got much of their domestic water from roof rainwater collection.

When you visit Dogslack Well you'll notice the piping is still in place and that's because this spring continued to supply water to the village up until 1938 when a spur pipe was built from the Thirlmere Aqueduct running 161 kms (100 miles) from Thirlmere Reservoir in the north of the Lake District all the way to Manchester.

Dogslack Well

If you're lucky enough to visit during the summer months Lambert's Meadow will be alive with wild flowers. It's owned and managed by the National Trust using traditional methods and is a wonderful spot on a sunny day to enjoy the butterflies and other insects buzzing around in the sunshine (if you visit after heavy rain be sure to wear your good boots as it can get boggy here).

Of course if you think a boggy field is a bit of challenge now, spare a thought for the folks of yesteryear who had the challenge of navigating the area before waymarked footpaths, wellies and Gore Tex™. In the late seventeenth century there was a big dispute involving the good Christian folk of Silverdale who had complained that the route between Silverdale and Warton was so treacherous that it was unreasonable to expect them to make the journey twice on Sundays and on all the feast days.

Lamberts Meadow view

The Church decided to settle the dispute by sending in an unbiased outsider – Rev James Fenton the Vicar of Lancaster – to make the journey and assess it himself. Unfortunately he didn't make it. Poor Rev Fenton got stranded in a bog and had to be rescued by locals, resulting in Silverdale finally getting their own vicar.

There have been a few famous names associated with Silverdale over the years – Charlotte and Emily Brontë passed their holidays at Cove House in the village (the founder of their school owned the house), and Elizabeth Gaskell – who published the first biography of Charlotte Brontë and the novel *Cranford* (on which the BBC TV series was based) – escaped from her home in Manchester to seek inspiration for her writing in the peaceful surroundings of Lindeth Tower (passed on the Jenny Brown's Point Walk – Walk 9).

The hall in the centre of the village, which plays a very active part in local village life, is named in honour of Elizabeth Gaskell. William Riley, another famous local author, helped to raise the funds for the building, which was built as a permanent home for the Silverdale Village Players amateur dramatics society.

The RSPB visitors' centre next to the car park at the start and end of the walk began life as Myers Farm – which is how it's still marked on OS Maps. The farm was originally built by Richard Thomas Gillow, the squire of nearby Leighton Hall. During the nineteenth century he drained the continually boggy Leighton Moss and created a large area of arable farmland (see Walk 3).

Leighton Moss reeds

The soil was incredibly fertile and the region was known as the 'Golden Bowl', supplying cereal crops to the local towns and, from 1857, using the Furness Railway to access markets further away. During World War One a lack of coal and manpower led to the pumps falling into disrepair and the area reflooding. After the war a drop in prices due to competition from international markets meant it was no longer economically viable to repair the pumps so crop production ceased.

The RSPB took over the running of what is now Leighton Moss in 1964 and they continue to restore and preserve the moss to support the wide variety of wildlife associated with it and encourage more to return. Today arable farming is rare on the thin limestone soils around the moss but, as you'll see from your walks, they provide an excellent habitat for sheep and cattle.

Sleepy sheep

Local tip: Throughout the summer months there is a series of Cross Bay Walks which anyone can join in. They start from either Arnside or Hest Bank and cross the sands to arrive in Kents Bank. All the walks are led by qualified guides and raise a lot of money for local and national charities – many of whom will lay on minibuses to get you to and from the start (check the internet for Morecambe Bay Cross Bay Walks). Although flat these walks are challenging so do be prepared – but they offer an unforgettable experience and the opportunity for a quick paddle or two.

Boardwalk around Hawes Water

WALK 5

Trowbarrow & Hawes Water

Start:	RSPB Leighton Moss Visitors' car park
Grid Ref:	SD 47642 75050
Distance:	7 km / 4.5 miles
Terrain:	Tarmac, hard track, forest track. A varied walk with some road walking at the start. Gentle ascents and one sharp descent through woodland
Parking:	Free car parking at Leighton Moss car park
Public Transport:	Silverdale train station 3 minutes' walk from start
Facilities:	Café and toilets in Leighton Moss visitors' centre

Overview

This is probably the best route for exploring the limestone in the area up close. The quarry face is well worth having a look at as there are fossilised corals in places. As you pass through Gait Barrows there are some great opportunities for scrambling over the crags, not to mention some superb spots for lunch.

Limestone pavement

Route

From the car park turn left and walk along road, away from the railway. (*If you prefer, you can cross into the RSPB visitors' centre and follow the way marked route from the back of the centre and alongside the road – when you emerge onto the road turn right and continue until you reach the gate.*) Continue for 300 m (¼ mile) until you reach a gate on the left signed 'Permissive Path Trowbarrow LNR' pass through the gate and bear slight right. Follow the wooded limestone gully, though the carabiner-style gate and woodland until you reach the quarry.

Keep left as you exit the woods and continue ahead until you reach the sandy track in the open quarry. Turn left along this track and, after 50 m, left again (within clear sight of the large boulder) to follow a broad gravel track which bears slight left and down into the woodland.

Remain on the path through the woods, passing the old limeworks, and continue on through the two gates to the lane. (**Point A**) Turn left along the lane, cross the railway bridge and continue to the road. Turn right and walk for a short distance until you reach a path on the right signed to Challan Hall.

Cross the stile and follow the field boundary then cross the railway with care. Continue on into Gait Barrows nature reserve, following the way marks towards Challen Hall. Beyond the kissing gate bear left when the path forks leading towards a small group of houses. Cross the stile adjacent to the gate and follow the driveway up to the road.

Carabiner gate

Turn right along the road and after approximately 50 m turn left through a farm gate (opposite the Silverdale village sign) to visit the Bowder Stone. When you return to the road bear left and cross it to follow the way marked path leading down into the woods on the far side. Remain on this path until you reach a signed path to the left which passes by a large old stone gate post. (**Point B**)

[*Exit point for short walk: remain on the path around Haweswater to* **Point C**.]

Follow this path through the woods and just before it reaches the road turn right. (*You can continue on across the road to follow the signed route to the edges of Silverdale Moss and some excellent views of Arnside Tower here if you wish, before returning to the route.*)

Remain on the woodland path, bearing right through a wall and ignoring any sharp forks or turns, until it joins a broad, hard track. Turn left here then right at the fork just before the green road barrier.

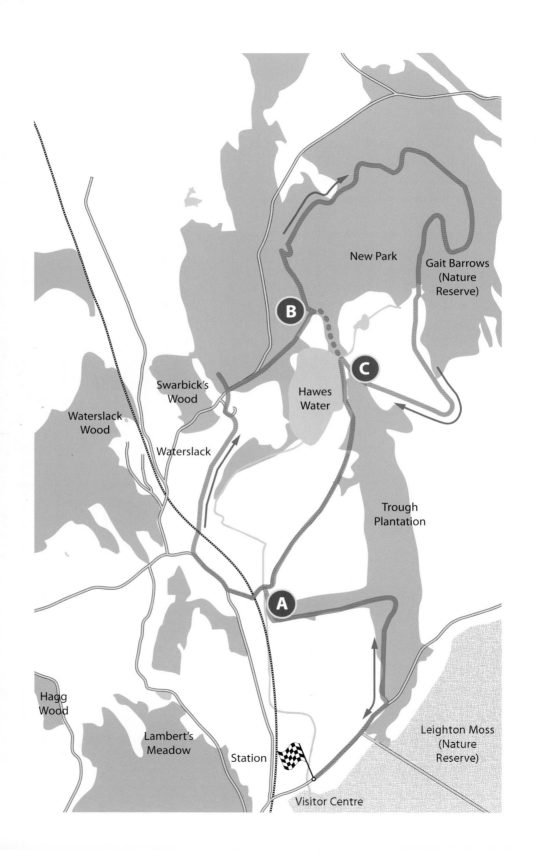

New Park

Gait Barrows
(Nature
Reserve)

B

C

Swarbick's
Wood

Waterslack
Wood

Hawes
Water

Waterslack

Trough
Plantation

A

Hagg
Wood

Lambert's
Meadow

Station

Leighton Moss
(Nature
Reserve)

Visitor Centre

Continue on this path until the purple arrow directs you to turn right into the woods. At the waymark numbered '2' turn left to reach an open limestone area. Continue ahead following the purple arrow on the far side leading slight right and then left at the next open area around onto another woodland path.

Continue on this path (do not turn left at waymark number '4') until you reach a broad gully with raised limestone on either side. At the end of the gully follow the waymark hard left to double back and along another gully. At the end drop down three steps (with rustic wooden handrail), then turn left to follow the path downhill (pausing to examine monument).

Silver Jubilee Memorial

Follow the path down and around to a gate. Go through the gate and swing left through an open field, then beyond across two more fields to a wall. Turn right in front of the wall to the information board, and then right again to follow the path down through two fields to a kissing gate in the bottom left hand corner.

Go through the gate and turn hard right. At the end of the boardwalk go through the gate on your left to reach another boardwalk running alongside the lake (**Point C**) and continue until you reach another gate at the far end. Pass through the gate and turn left. Follow the path as turns into road then continue on along the road until you reach to the Trowbarrow permissive path on the left. (**Point A**)

Retrace your steps back through the woodland and the quarry to return to the start of the walk. (*Note: for variety you can turn left at the Limeworks and follow the short track through the woods, turning left when you rejoin the main track. You can also take the opportunity on the return journey to visit and explore the quarry in greater detail.*)

Limeworks infoboard

A tale about rare plants, inspiration and high adrenaline

Scotland has Nessie and Hawes Water has a giant eel. Or snake. Or some sort of giant serpent anyway. Of course no-one has ever seen it, that would just spoil the fun, but the evidence is right there to see. Just to the north of the lake is Challan Farm and beyond that you'll see the 'Bowk Stone' marked on the map, known locally as the Buck Stone, Bowder Stone or Rocking Stone. In reality it's most likely to be a glacial boulder left behind when the ice retreated but to the locals it was the sleeping place of the eel.

Allegedly, the eel used to curl itself around the base of the rock, causing the groove underneath the boulder we can see today. There it would snooze until a hapless sheep wandered too close, at which point it would snap up the sheep and carry it off to the depths of the lake for dinner.

Hawes Water

Hawes Water itself is a geologically interesting lake. It's around 12.5 m deep and technically it's a 'doline' (more commonly called 'sink hole') which is a basin-shaped lake formed by the acidic erosive activity of water. The base is full of calcareous sediments from the limestone mixed in with rich peaty organic matter from the reeds and is surprisingly, given its modest size, the largest naturally occurring lake in Lancashire.

In between the huge limestone beds are thick beds of clays and silts and, as with the limestone, these were put to good use. If you take a look at a map of Silverdale you'll notice 'Potter Hill' just to the east of the village – this is the site of a number of late medieval kilns. Many pieces of ancient pottery have been unearthed during the building of houses and extensions in the area, much of it glazed and most of it appearing to come from basins or bowls.

The clay for this pottery is thought to have been sourced from the area around Hawes Water and 'clay holes' can still be found marked on older maps, though they are hard to find today as the area is now much overgrown. Fragments of this pottery have been found as far afield as Cockersands Abbey and Eskdale, allowing us to map the trading routes of these early entrepreneurs.

Lady's slipper orchid

Gait Barrows bench

The section of the walk through Gait Barrows is probably the best place for getting a good close up view of limestone pavement. Its bench is perfect for pausing on for lunch or a quick snack and while you're sitting there take a good look down inside the deep cracks, known as grikes, where you'll find an abundance of interesting ferns and plants. During the spring you may also be lucky enough to spot the incredibly rare lady's slipper orchid – once thought to be extinct in the UK but slowly coming back thanks to the careful management of the land.

Trowbarrow Quarry

The characteristic patterns across the top of the limestone are referred to as runnels, pits and pans and are simply formed by water erosion. The Wildlife and Countryside Protection Act of 1981 made it illegal to remove limestone pavement but prior to then huge chunks were commonly taken away and used to decorate local gardens and driveways.

Trowbarrow Quarry, which dominates the start and end of the walk, has a wonderful 'secret garden' feel to it. As you approach along the narrow, shadowy trough there are few clues to the bright, open quarry that awaits. The name 'Trowbarrow' comes from the Middle English word 'trow' meaning 'trough', and the Anglo-Saxon 'bærwe' which translates as 'barrow' or 'grove'. The hill that was once nearby has now been largely quarried away.

The quarry opened in 1857, as did the local line of the Furness railway, and the two events are closely linked. Prior to then there was no economically viable way to move the limestone but that all changed with the advent of the railways and, once it began, the quarrying continued here for around 100 years. At the limeworks, just down from the quarry, there was once a large limekiln and this is where they first combined limestone with bitumen to produce tarmacadam, though back then it was called Quarrite.

As you wander around the quarry on a warm summer's day it's hard to imagine what it must have been like during that time. These days the place is awash with birds, butterflies and dragonflies. There's a

Shelter stone

huge stone in the centre of the quarry known as the 'Shelter Stone' as it's where the workmen would shelter when blasting was taking place. Today it could more appropriately be known as 'climbing stone' as it attracts bouldering enthusiasts and their tell-tale chalk handprints can usually be found on the rock.

The sheer cliff faces are also popular with climbers which explains why the gate at the entrance is shaped like a climber's carabiner. There are around 120 climbing routes in the quarry of varying difficulty and with a variety of interesting names, though 'Essence of Giraffe' and 'Diary of a Sane Man' are perhaps the most colourful.

These days the quarry is managed by Arnside Area of Outstanding Natural Beauty using traditional methods such as coppicing and grazing and the wonderful variety of insects, animals and plants – including the beautiful and rare bee orchid – are testimony to their success. It's always worth taking a look at their website as they offer a range of interesting and engaging family activities throughout the year.

Climbers

Bee orchid

Pepperpot

WALK 6

Middlebarrow

Start:	National Trust car park, Park Road Silverdale
Grid Ref:	SD 47124 75936
Distance:	6.5 km / 4 miles
Terrain:	Forest track. A particularly family friendly walk with no road walking and only gentle ascents and descents.
Parking:	Free car parking in National Trust car park
Public Transport:	Short walk from Silverdale station, also served by Silverdale Shuttle bus.
Facilities:	No facilities on the route.

Overview

This is the perfect walk for a hot summer's day when you'll really appreciate the cool shade of the woodland. It offers a good balance of manmade and natural points of interest and most children will enjoy scrambling over the limestone pavement around the Pepperpot.

Camping pods

Route

From the car park go through the kissing gate and up into Eaves wood. At the T junction turn right to follow the route signposted to Waterslack. Stay on the path as it joins a bigger path and winds through the woodland to the edge of the quarry.

Turn right to follow the small green waymarks which will lead you down and alongside the railway line to the quarry entrance. Continue

straight on with the railway on your right (*do not* go over the crossing). **(Point A)**

Where the path forks, bear left to follow the route signposted to Arnside Tower and follow it all the way to the top of the woods. Pass through the gate to follow the tractor tracks up the field with Arnside Tower on your left. After visiting the tower

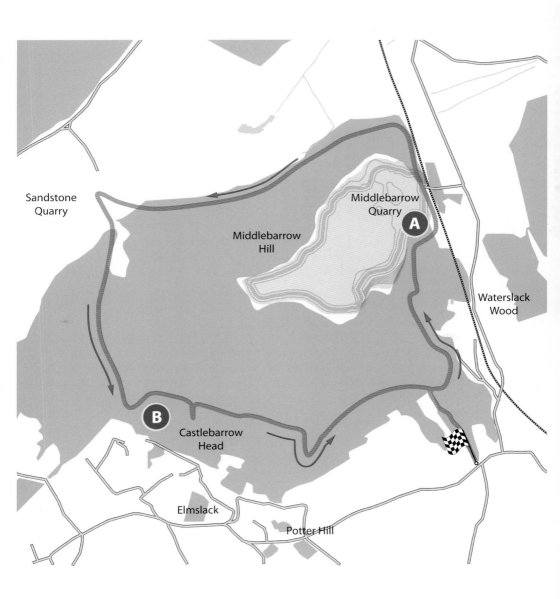

Sandstone
Quarry

Middlebarrow
Quarry

A

Middlebarrow
Hill

Waterslack
Wood

B

Castlebarrow
Head

Elmslack

Potter Hill

Old cottage

continue following the tracks until you reach a signpost – take the route left to Eaves Wood over the large ladder stile and keep right at the fork.

Follow the path up to a kissing gate into Holgates Caravan Park and keep to the waymarked route across the site to reach the path leading up into the trees on the far side. Remain on this path to reach a gap in the wall, go through this gap and take the path immediately on your left. (**Point B**)

Continue on past the NT Eaves wood sign, climbing a little then, just beyond some rough limestone steps, take the small path on the right leading away from the wall and into the woods. When the path levels and the woods open out there are numerous paths to choose from. Keep towards the right hand side as you cross the open area and continue until you reach the 'Pepperpot' memorial.

Take the path leading away behind the 'Pepperpot' dropping down and to the right then continue on following waymarked 'P' signs until you reach a large intersection of paths.

Turn left here towards 'Beech Circle'. Keep right at the first fork and then left at the second (passing the remains of a cottage in the woods to your left) and remain on the path to reach an old set of gateposts at a T junction. Turn right here then immediately left to return to the car park.

A tale about trees and towers

These days woodland walks are usually a leisurely and enjoyable activity, but long before the good folks of Arnside and Silverdale AONB were maintaining nice clear footpaths for us, things would have been challenging. Before there were proper paths and roads chances are that if you weren't wading through a bog you'd probably be fighting your way through the woodland.

Over the years the woodlands have been worked extensively to support the local communities and there is evidence of coppicing in many places (see the trees along the Fairy Steps route) which would have provided wood for building, bobbins and tools. Typically hazel was coppiced as it produces nice straight poles which can easily be put to use in lots of different ways. The nuts too would have been welcome in the autumn – as would the cherries from the local cherry trees – once revered as some of the finest in the country. (Cherry trees are easy to spot, tall, straight and with distinctive banding around the trunk.)

Arnside Tower silhouette

Cherry tree trunk

In a landscape full of breathtaking views the three main features on this route are all manmade. First up is Middlebarrow Quarry, clearly not an attractive feature but another example of man making his mark on the landscape. Where we once used the woodlands for materials so Middlebarrow Quarry was created to quarry limestone for building, farming etc. The quarry has been closed since 2002 due to the depth it reached and the potential impact on the local water table.

It's advisable to keep well away from the walls which are unstable enough to put off the local climbers. At one point there was talk of it being redeveloped as an ecofriendly conference centre but for now it is being left to return to nature – old quarries often make excellent nature reserves with the sheer and inaccessible walls proving popular with birds such as peregrines.

The next structure is rather more attractive: Arnside Tower. The precise date it was built isn't known but the first mention of it is in a document dating from 1517 which, even then, states it was 'worth nothing yearly'. The tower is probably a Pele tower, something unique to this part of the world. The towers were typically (though not always) built for defence where a family could hole themselves up to survive a siege and were built in response to the repeated attacks from the border reivers (Scottish raiders) to the north. The ground floor would have been for animals and storage with the living quarters on the floors above.

Arnside Tower was badly burned in 1602 but was repaired and continued to be lived in until 1684 when it was dismantled, with parts of it used in other local structures, as was common practice at the time. In 1777 the local history society reported 'the walls thereof

Arnside Tower

not much decayed' but that wasn't to last. During 1884 a violent storm blew down a large part of the remaining structure and left us with something like what we see today. What makes Arnside a particularly interesting Pele tower is that it is free standing – many others were incorporated into larger manorial buildings or farms (see Hazelslack Tower in Walk 1).

Just down the road from Arnside Tower you'll find Hollins Farm (not on the walk route) with farm buildings dating back to 1771. The name 'Hollins' is derived from the growth of holly 'haggs' for use as sheep feed in the winter. It's common practice to bring the sheep down from the high hills and allow them to winter in protected valleys and return to the hills after lambing.

Pepperpot and Morecambe Bay

Further along the walk is the third manmade structure. Known locally as 'The Pepperpot', it was built to commemorate the Golden Jubilee of Queen Victoria in 1887. There have been plans over the years to build a 'salt cellar' to accompany it (most recently in 1977 to commemorate Queen Elizabeth's Silver Jubilee) but nothing has so far materialised – you will, however, find a Silver Jubilee memorial on the Trowbarrow walk (Walk 5) which was unveiled in Gait Barrows nature reserve to commemorate both the jubilee and the recognition of Gait Barrows as a National Nature Reserve.

Beech circle

The views from here out across Morecambe Bay are spectacular and it's the perfect spot to watch the sunset and listen to the owls as they come out and begin their evening hunt.

Eaves Wood as we see it today is largely down to one man, Thomas Inman, who during the nineteenth century owned and managed the estate, using some areas for coppicing and some areas as ornamental gardens. The Beech Circle towards the end of the walk is evidence of some of his experimental planting; whilst common across the south of England, the beech tree is comparatively rare this far north.

The building remains in the woods nearby were once a gamekeeper's cottage (though a layer of cockleshells found on the floor suggests it was also once occupied by a fisherman). Today you can wander around what's left of it, perhaps plotting your own self sufficient *Grand Designs* project for a life away from it all surrounded by beautiful woodland.

Morecambe Bay sunset

Local tip: There are only around 380 breeding pairs of marsh harriers in the whole country so it's an absolute privilege to see them at Leighton Moss. If you're patient you can usually spot one on most visits but do ask any of the wardens when you arrive and they'll tell you the best hide to visit to see them on any given day. If you visit during the spring months and you're really lucky you might even catch one of their amazing sky dances. Leighton Moss is particularly interesting during the autumn and winter months when you can spot rare species such as bearded tits and bitterns – usually from Causeway Hide – or enjoy a spectacular starling murmuration.

WALK 7

Yealand Hall Allotments

Start:	Lay-by at Thrang Brow Lane/Storrs Lane
Grid Ref:	SD 49388 76100
Distance:	7 km / 4.5 miles
Terrain:	Hard track, fields, tarmac. A relatively flat walk with plenty of woodland stretches. Paths clearly marked but may be overgrown in places.
Parking:	Free car parking in lay-by
Public Transport:	Silverdale station 3.2 km (2 miles) from the start of the walk.
Facilities:	None along the route.

Overview

This walk has a lovely, long, gentle lead in along the woodland track at the start. There are some excellent viewpoints from the limestone crags towards the end of the walk — well worth the short detour. In the section of the walk near old Leighton Beck Furnace, look for the sparkly 'clinker' still lining the path.

Route

From the lay-by go through the gap in the wall and along the short path. Turn right to join the main track and remain on it as it winds through the woodland, bearing right at the fork to reach a wooden gate.

[*Exit point for short walk: go through the gate and turn right to reach* **Point C**.]

Go through the gate and turn left to follow an enclosed path. Just before you reach the next wooden gate turn right to cross a stile (**Point A**), following a path up into woodland. Remain on this path to cross another stile then continue on through the field, bearing slight left at the top to follow the waymarkers around the trees to a metal gate and stile.

Cross the stile and bear slight right across the field, looking for the waymarkers around the edges of the trees. Follow the faint path as it continues to a stone stile. Cross the stile and continue slight left across the next field to the wooden kissing gate in the left hand corner.

Go through the kissing gate and follow the obvious yellow waymarkers across the field to another stile. Continue on, following the clear waymarkers, across two more fields until you reach the road. **(Point B)**

Cross the road and continue straight on over small bridge. Follow the lane as it passes the houses then rises gradually to the woodland. At the crest of the hill take the track to the left signed Dollywood Lane. Remain on this enclosed track as it gently descends through the woodland.

When the woodland on the left ends continue to the end of the field and look for a narrow wooden stile through the hedge near to a wooden gate. Cross the stile and continue across the field to the small wooden bridge on the far side. After the bridge bear hard left along the beck before veering slightly to the right to pass through a disused gate then continue on with the field boundary on your immediate right.

Bear right in the next field and continue to follow the farm track through another field and around up to the road (near to **Point B**). (*Turn right here to visit the commemorative plaque on the wall of the small driveway.*) Turn left along the road and continue on, towards Carnforth, until you reach a clear waymarked path on your right, signed to Hawes Water and Yealand Storrs.

Cross the stile and follow the waymarked route straight ahead, crossing three fields to reach a metal gate. Go through the gate and continue on the clear path, through the woodland to reach another wooden gate **(Point C)**. Go through the gate and turn immediately left to follow the small track.

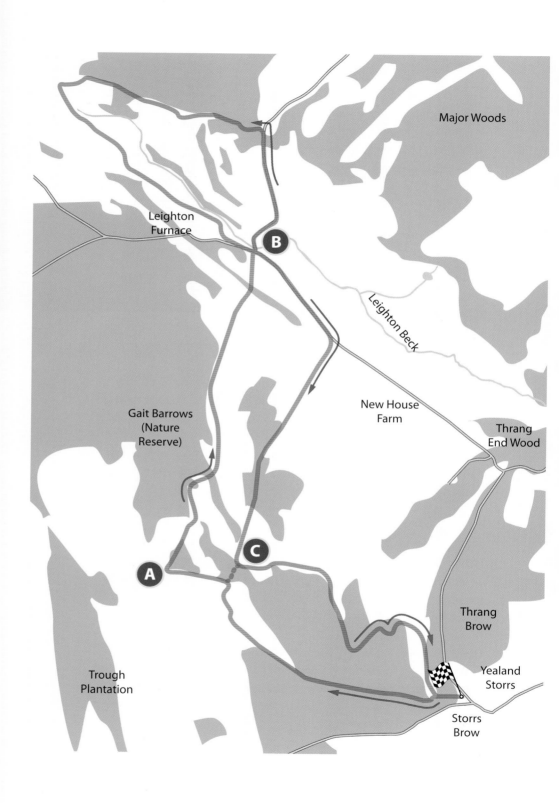

Pass through the kissing gate and remain on the path as it climbs gently and curves right to skirt the edge of the woodland. Follow the path through the next kissing gate and downhill. As you reach the left hand field boundary, take the left fork leading up and around to the left to another kissing gate.

Remain on this route, ignoring any forks leading into the woods, until it starts to descend, at this point look for a white waymarker leading right to a view point on a small limestone crag. From the crag return to the path, following it downhill until it rejoins the broad track. Turn left to return to the start of the walk.

A tale about giant furnaces not giant marrows

First of all, don't expect the start of this walk to be awash with prize marrows and cucumbers – the term 'allotment' in this case refers to the historic definition – a parcel of land given ('allotted') by the government for the use by local people. The practice dates back to Anglo-Saxon times (around AD 400 through to 1066) and not all of the land was used for growing crops – some was allocated in strips to local households while other areas remained communal or waste land.

Meadow brown butterfly

The name 'Yealand' most likely comes from the Anglo-Saxon words for High Land and the prominent limestone hillside offers superb views down over Leighton Moss and out towards Morecambe Bay. There are also plenty of opportunities for equally superb views of wildlife including both roe and fallow deer – your best chances are either at dusk or dawn during spring and autumn, but you'll need to be quiet and leave the dog at home.

This walk also offers great views of the lowland areas, many of which were used for peat production. Peat was the main fuel of the area and was typically cut in May and stacked to dry ready for burning come the autumn. The best stuff was usually a few feet down so the strips tended to be quite deep and if you look carefully at some of the local fields you can still just about make out the characteristic straight lines of the old strips.

The limestone and the peat, together with the woodland and a ready water supply, are behind a major piece of industry in the area. In the early eighteenth century a furnace was built at Leighton Beck by the Backbarrow Company. All that remains now is a commemorative plaque and a few spoil heaps, and if you look carefully at the river you can make out where the mill pond once was (additional structures have also been detected just below the surface using the same LIDAR technology that's being used around Warton Crag – see Walk 8).

The iron ore was brought in from across Morecambe Bay via Arnside and the building of the furnace was not without controversy. At that time there were concerns that too many English woodlands were being destroyed to fuel iron works but one thing Leighton Beck had going for it was its peat – according to one of the most detailed accounts (the *History of Warton Parish* by John Lucas) the peat not only spared the woodland, it also produced better iron, although in reality the furnace was fired by a combination of wood, charcoal and peat.

Limestone scenery

Furnace plaque

Iron smelting requires very high temperatures (>1000°C) and getting the furnace up to temperature could take three to four weeks but, once there, it would operate night and day for many months or even years. The furnace operated until 1806 when it was badly damaged by an explosion and was never rebuilt. The charcoal barn and iron store survived and now form part of the nearby farm buildings and, if you're feeling fanciful, take a look at the large iron farm gates you pass on the way to Dollywood Lane – we have no evidence to link them to the furnace, but it's awfully tempting…

Once you've finished the walk cross the road to stand by the white metal fence looking down across Leighton Moss (be careful; it's a narrow verge) and you'll get a sense of some interesting aspects of the history of the area. Down in Storrs Moss (below and to your right) was found the earliest evidence for man in the area. In the 1960s archaeologists from Liverpool University dug out a wooden structure

Iron gates

from deep under the moss together with fragments of flint – the oldest elements were dated to 4200 BC – and the owners of nearby Browfoot Farm have often discovered Stone Age items when working the land, most of which are now in Kendal Museum.

You may also notice that the field directly in front of you is far from smooth and flat. It's likely that Yealand Storrs was once a much larger community, sitting at an important road junction on the ancient west coast route to Scotland but was decimated either by the Black Death, Scottish raids or a combination of the two. Although it's never been excavated it's thought that the lumps in the field may possibly be the buried remains of the old village, though this is far from certain – if anyone has the number for *Time Team*, now's the time to call them and tempt them back out of retirement.

Yealand sunset

WALK 8

Warton Crag

Start:	RSPB Quaker's Stang car park
Grid Ref:	SD 47565 73729
Distance:	8 km / 5 miles
Terrain:	Tarmac, hard track, forest track. The first half of the walk is a long, gentle, uphill, followed by glorious views and a long, gentle, downhill.
Parking:	Free car parking at Quaker's Stang car park
Public Transport:	Silverdale train station 1.6 km (1 mile) from the start of the walk.
Facilities:	None on route, café and toilets in Leighton Moss visitors' centre 1.6 km away

Overview

This is a walk of two halves, an uphill half and a downhill half, with magnificent views from Warton Crag in the middle. Much of this route follows ancient lanes and coach roads and as you wander along them, it's interesting to imagine what it must have been like when the old mail coaches came thundering through.

Warton Crag view

Route

From the car park follow the track back to the road and turn right. Continue along the pavement to Moss House Farm and bear left to follow the road rising sharply uphill (Signed to Carnforth & Warton). After 500 m (¼ mile) take the track to the left signposted 'Public Bridleway' (Occupation Road) and follow it uphill. After 800 m (½ mile) the track levels out slightly – look for a large wooden gate on your right with a gap stile and a 'no horses' sign (**Point A**) – pass through the stile and follow the broad track as it winds through the woodland. Continue ahead through a kissing gate and remain on the track as it climbs gently through woods to reach the beacon. Go past the beacon, to the crags, to admire the view.

Return back to the beacon and take the path passing behind it, past the trig point, and follow it downhill – there are various stopping off points along the way which each offer a different view over Morecambe Bay and Lancaster. Just beyond the lowermost viewpoint the track swings away from the edge of the crags – fork left here and

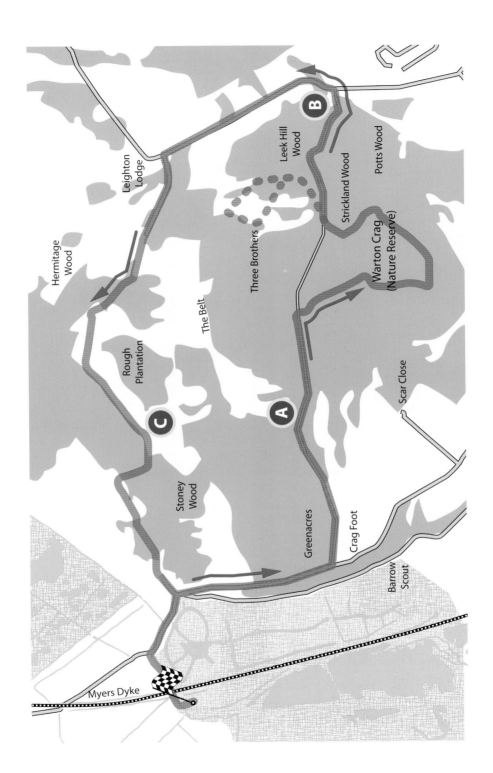

Myers Dyke

Hermitage Wood

Leighton Lodge

Leek Hill Wood

Three Brothers

Strickland Wood

Potts Wood

The Belt

Warton Crag (Nature Reserve)

Rough Plantation

Stoney Wood

Scar Close

Greenacres

Crag Foot

Barrow Scout

A

B

C

Glacial erratic

continue around and down through the woods. When you meet a larger track at a T junction turn right and remain on the path heading downhill, then keep left at the fork by the large oak tree to return back to the broad walled track.

Turn right along the track – just ahead on the left is a signed route to the Three Brothers (a group of standing stones) which is worth the short detour – and remain on the track until you reach the road. (**Point B**) Turn left following the road slightly uphill then just before the road bears sharp right turn left following a signed route to Crag Foot. Continue ahead along the broad track, crossing a gate adjacent to a large metal gate.

Continue along the field boundary, as the broad track swings left, drop down to the right to cross a stile and follow the path downhill through the woodland. As you emerge from the trees bear slight right to walk diagonally down across the field to a metal gate and stile in the far corner. Cross into the next field, keeping to the right hand field boundary. (**Point C**)

Continue following the boundary of the woodland until you arrive at another metal gate – pass through this gate and bear right to follow the track as it winds down hill through a large field, with excellent views of Leighton Moss (the Golden Bowl). After the gated stile at the bottom of this field bear right into the woods.

At the hard track turn right and remain on this track as it turns left between the farm buildings and returns to the main road. Turn right to retrace your steps back to the car park.

Early purple orchid

A tale about ancient forts and mysterious holes

At 163 m (535 ft) Warton Crag is the highest point in the Arnside & Silverdale Area of Outstanding Natural Beauty and, as soon as you reach the top of the crag, you can understand why our Iron Age ancestors would have built a fort here. Today we stand back and admire the views but back then those views, and the opportunities they gave for spotting potential marauders, would have made the place prime real estate.

The main track up and over the crag, Occupation Road, is an old Drover's road along which cattle and other livestock were driven back in the days before refrigeration when the only way to ensure fresh meat was to buy it while it was still living and breathing. A possible origin for the unusual name is that it was a lane used every day by estate workers – those with an 'occupation' – who needed to get to work.

Warton Crag itself is a glorious limestone cliff rich in a variety of rare flora and fauna and so special that as well as being a Site of Special Scientific interest (SSSI) it is owned and managed by four different organisations who work together to ensure the rare habitats are protected and maintained. (RSPB, Lancashire Wildlife Trust, Lancashire City Council and Lancashire County Council.)

There's not much of the Iron Age Hill Fort left to see on top of Warton Crag, but there's some amazing work currently being commissioned by Whitecross Archaeology Group and Morecambe Bay Partnership (MBP) which will hopefully tell us a lot more than we already know. The fort is a scheduled ancient monument and is described as being 'multivallate' which simply means it has more than one defensive boundary – in this case the main fort sat on top of the hill with the defensive boundaries surrounding it to the north east.

The remains of the fort are very hard to see with an untrained eye but LIDAR surveys currently being undertaken by MBP (the same idea as RADAR but using lasers instead of radio waves) are penetrating through the woodland and undergrowth and revealing what remains of the layout, allowing the various groups managing the site to determine the best conservation approach and ensure it doesn't get lost forever.

The hillside is littered with a number of holes and caves – some natural and some manmade. The most well known are the Dog Holes towards the start of the walk (now on private land). During an excavation in the early twentieth century, human and animal remains

Roe deer

Harry Hest Hole

were found which dated back to the Neolithic Period (4000–2500 BC). The excavation also discovered Roman pottery indicating a prolonged period of use for the caves and it's evident from postcards that the caves were a popular place to visit during the Victorian era, with local folklore suggesting they were used as a hideout for a highwayman and his horse.

On the top of Warton Crag you can sit and enjoy views of Morecambe Bay, but watch where you sit if you're a newlywed – Bride's Chair is a rocky outcrop not far from the summit where brides have traditionally sat after their wedding day as a fertility ritual (or to ensure a long and happy life if you read some of the slightly more prudish Victorian texts).

When you look down onto Morecambe Bay from the top of the crag you're looking at the old main road across the sands. The route was, and still is, treacherous and many lives have been lost over the years thanks to the quick sands and even quicker tides.

Warton Crag

Saltmarsh

You may wonder why people would even attempt it when it's so dangerous. Well, at the time the alternative was just as risky; if you were crossing the bay you faced around 12 km (7.5 miles) of dangerous sands and tides compared to over 45 km (28 miles) of dangerous bogs and mires if you took the inland route. Hiring a local guide was great if you could afford it, but even then still no guarantee of survival and coaches as well as individuals often failed to make the crossing. In 1907 one ancient mariner, clearly having been involved in one rescue too many, was asked how many guides had been lost crossing the bay. 'I never knew any lost,' he said. 'There's one or two drowned, now and again, but they're generally found when the tide goes out.'

These days if you want to cross the sands you can take part in one of the many 'Cross Bay Walks' organised throughout the summer months. These challenging walks raise a huge amount of money for local charities and are a fantastic opportunity to see Morecambe Bay safely and from a completely new angle.

Avocets

Local tip: If the weather takes a turn for the worse, or if you just fancy finding out more about the local history, then pay a visit to Lancaster – it's a short drive or there are regular trains from Arnside and Silverdale. Lancaster Castle offers a superb guided tour with lots of grisly anecdotes from its long and fascinating history, from the Pendle Witch trials to the many executions which took place there. It is still used today as a Crown Court and, if the court is not in session, the tour will take you through the imposing courtroom. Throughout the year there are also a number of festivals in the city celebrating local food, music and art – check the Visit Lancashire website to see what's on during your visit.

Silverdale Cove from cave

WALK 9

Jenny Brown's Point

Start:	RSPB Quaker's Stang car park
Grid Ref:	SD 47565 73729
Distance:	8 km / 5 miles
Terrain:	Hard track, beach, tarmac, forest. A relatively flat but challenging walk. The beach sections can be unpredictable and there's a small scramble up a limestone crag (with a work around if you don't fancy it).
Parking:	Free car parking at Quaker's Stang car park
Public Transport:	Silverdale train station 1.6 km (1 mile) from the start of the walk.
Facilities:	Wolfhouse Café and 2 pubs along the route. Route also passes very close to Silverdale village centre.

Overview

We did think of tweaking this route to avoid the more challenging sections, but sometimes it's good to do something a bit different. The beach section around to Silverdale Cove is harder work than a forest track, and the scramble up the limestone cliff at Woodwell is a lot easier than it looks, with clear and easy steps – though we have included a diversion if you prefer.

Silverdale Cove

Route

Return to the entrance of the car park and follow the route clearly signed 'Lancashire Coastal Way'. Remain on the raised embankment (Quaker's Stang) to a footpath intersection at the base of the hill. Cross the stile and take the path left, towards Jenny Brown's Point. **(Point A)**

Continue round shore to the single-track road just beyond the houses. After passing the small quarry on your right take the kissing gate on your left to Jack Scout and keep to the main track until you reach a gate. After the gate bear left at the fork until you reach a small cove then continue on, uphill and straight on then follow the fence on your left above the beach. Just before you reach a stile in the fence, bear right at a fork towards a large stone bench, forking left further on to reach it.

Loop around the left hand side and up behind the bench and continue on the grassy track towards the dry stone wall – just before you reach the wall bear left to the lime kiln. Keep to the path leading left around the back of the kiln and up onto the lane. Turn left and continue on and passing Lindeth Tower on your left. **(Point B)**

[*Exit point for short walk: once you've passed the farm there is a small road that leads to the right, Hollins Lane, turn right and follow the road past The Wolfhouse Café until you see a sign to the right directing you to Quaker's Stang. Follow the signed route back to* **Point A**.]

Continue along Lindeth Road until you reach the junction then turn left and continue down to the tidal car park.

(Warning: path along shore may have tide restrictions; check tide time and take extra care on slippery rocks. Don't be tempted to walk out onto the soft sand at low tide.)

Lindeth Tower

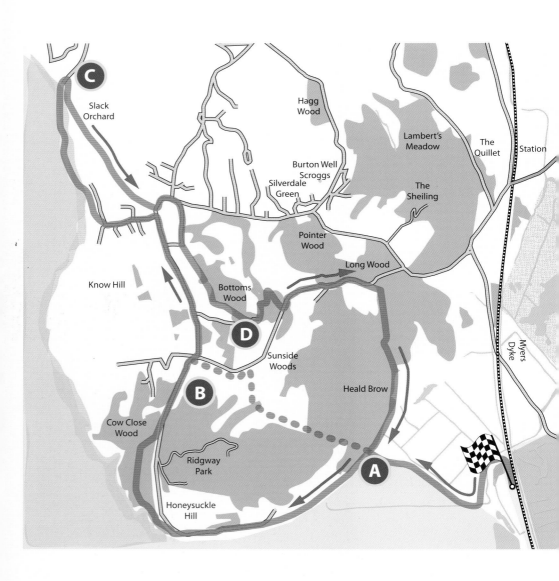

C

Slack
Orchard

Hagg
Wood

Lambert's
Meadow

The
Quillet

Station

Burton Well
Scroggs

Silverdale
Green

The
Sheiling

Know Hill

Pointer
Wood

Bottoms
Wood

Long Wood

D

Sunside
Woods

Heald Brow

Myers
Dyke

B

Cow Close
Wood

Ridgway
Park

Honeysuckle
Hill

A

Head out around the shore until you reach Silverdale Cove with its distinctive round cave in the cliff face. From the back of the cove turn right to follow the higher path back along the cliff tops signed 'The Lots Shore Road' **(Point C)** – follow the way marked route across the fields.

Once at the road, turn left and follow it up to the junction, continue in the direction signposted Carnforth and after 20 m take the small track on the right, signposted Woodwell.

Follow this waymarked track along the backs of houses and into woodland, until you reach an opening in the wall signed NT Bottoms Wood on your left, cross into the woods bearing right to follow the path and right again at the end to arrive at a small car park.

Cross the car park and follow the route left to The Green via Cliff Path. At the top of the limestone steps turn left then bear right down through the woods to join the main track. Go left through a kissing gate and up a small hill then right at the top to cross a field to Hollins Lane.

(*Note: if you don't fancy the limestone scramble, go right at Woodwell towards Hollins Lane, then double back just before the gate to follow the cliff path back to the kissing gate.*)

Turn left along the lane and follow it past Hazelwood Hall until you reach a track on the right with an old sign reading The Shore and Browns Point. Follow the path through the woodland to return to the stile at Quaker's Stang then turn left to follow the embankment back to the car park.

A tale about beautiful beaches and grandiose plans

If we were writing this walking guide 320 million years ago we'd be describing warm, tropical seas with crystal clear waves breaking along a bleached white beach while the sun beats down from a cloudless sky. Beyond the edges of the beach would be miles of thick, lush, forest; beautiful but devoid of birdsong.

Back in the Carboniferous, when the rocks around here were laid down, Britain was lounging somewhere near the equator. At Jenny Brown's Point the warm shallow lagoons, teeming with shellfish and corals, created the limestone we can see along much of this walk (and the others in the book) while further north the thick forests created the coal mined up at Workington and Whitehaven. The first reptiles appeared on earth during this time period, but you'd have to wait another 160 million years or so for the birds to appear.

Silverdale Cove

Chimney at Jenny Brown's Point

Today, two main features dominate the start of this walk: Quaker's Stang – the large embankment you follow along the first stretch – and the chimney on the beach. The large chimney is commonly, though not universally, thought to be the remains of a copper smelting works. Copper and iron were mined in the region during the nineteenth century and the remains of a small jetty (visible at low tide) suggest it was possibly removed by ship. There is currently a major project underway to establish exactly what the chimney was used for so if you want to follow the mystery as it unravels keep your eye on Morecambe Bay Partnership's website.

The origins of the curiously named Quaker's Stang are hard to pin down but the most recent research by the Mourholme Local History Society has found that the term Quaker's Stang was used to refer to the stone bridge crossed at the start of the walk. That said, there's a history of Quakers in the area going back to the seventeenth century and 'stang' is a word of Scandinavian origin meaning 'rod' or 'pole' relating to a unit of measurement – so it's possible that 'Quaker's Stang' was simply a measured area of land belonging to the Quakers.

It's also been suggested that the name is a corruption of Quicksand Pool which, despite its name, is the rivulet which runs from under the bridge and meets the bank at each end. It's now thought the raised bank was constructed sometime during the 1820s as it's listed on an 1829 land sales map as 'The New Embankment' – they certainly built things to last back then!

Garlic woods

Saltmarsh patterns

Jenny Brown's Point is popularly said to be named after a nanny who drowned trying to save her charges from a rising tide during the eighteenth century, but this is far from certain. Recent research (again, carried out by the Mourholme Society) has identified that in 1671 a woman called Jenny Brown was named as a beneficiary in a will and lived in Dykehouse Farm next to Brown's Houses near to the chimney; though it's still not completely clear why the point would then have been named after her.

The views from Jenny Brown's Point sweep down across the vast expanse of Morecambe Bay. The greatest loss of life there in a single incident occurred just off Jenny Brown's Point on 3 September 1894 when The Matchless, a tourist boat carrying passengers from Morecambe for a day trip to Grange-over-Sands, was caught by a rogue gust of wind and capsized just off the coast. 25 people lost their lives including 13 from the town of Burnley (Morecambe was a popular holiday spot for mill workers and that particular week was the holiday week for Burnley).

Just beyond Jenny Brown's Point is a quarry on your right and, to your left, the remains of a stone embankment stretching out into the sands. This is all that's left of an early attempt to enclose a huge chunk of the bay and reclaim it for agricultural use. In the 1870s Herbert John Walduck bought up 10,000 acres of the local land with the intention of adding an additional 6,000 acres by enclosing and reclaiming all the land between Arnside Point and Hest Bank (just north of Morecambe). His initial application was overturned due to ancient grazing rights but a secondary application for the smaller area between Jenny Brown's Point and Hest Bank was successful.

Group walk and below,
Jack Scout bench

Work began on the embankment using stone from the quarry opposite, but was abandoned in 1885 for financial reasons. The houses near the chimney were used by the navvies working on the wall and rather than sleep in dormitories, Walduck partitioned the house so that 40 men each had their own room.

The remainder of the path to Silverdale may appear peaceful and pretty but beware; you are walking in the footsteps of Vikings! In September 2011 a collection of over 200 items (known as the Silverdale Hoard) was found in a field not far from the village. The find was made up of assorted coins, ingots and jewellery all dated to around AD 900, and although no-one is sure quite why they were buried (perhaps for safe keeping by someone fated never to return from war). The variety and decorations of the pieces has given us a valuable insight into Viking life.

We may no longer enjoy the warm tropical seas of the Carboniferous era, but we can at least enjoy the huge variety of birds that have come along since then. Once you've finished the walk pay a visit to the RSPB hides, accessible from the far side of the car park. There, depending on the time of year, you can enjoy watching gulls, geese, curlew, oyster catchers, avocets and many more as you finish off the final bit of tea in your flask.

WALK 10

Warton

Start:	Warton Crag Nature Reserve car park
Grid Ref:	SD 49151 72367
Distance:	7 km / 4.5 miles
Terrain:	Forest track, tarmac, fields. A sharp climb at the start is rewarded with excellent views. The remainder of the walk is low level with clear and solid paths throughout.
Parking:	Free car parking at Warton Crag car park
Public Transport:	None
Facilities:	Pubs in Warton village and Millhead.

Overview

This is the most 'towny' of all the walks and, in some ways, the least picturesque, but it does cover a lot of really interesting historical places. The best views are at the start from the top of the quarry – so make sure you have your camera ready.

Warton

Route

As you face the main quarry, take the path to the left into the woodland (opposite the stone wall). As you make your way up through the woodland, keep taking the right hand forks until you emerge onto the top of the quarry – keep away from the edge! Continue along the path as it crosses the top of the quarry, go through a kissing gate and remain on the path as it descends along the limestone layers.

Eagle bench

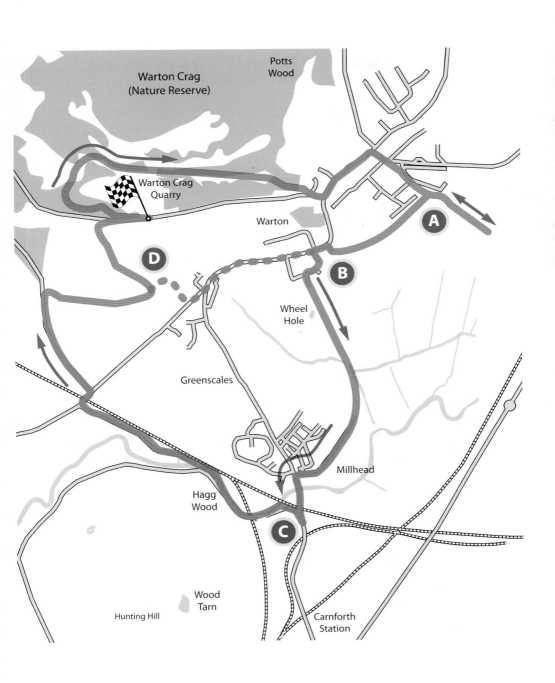

Warton Crag
(Nature Reserve)

Potts
Wood

Warton Crag
Quarry

Warton

A

D

B

Wheel
Hole

Greenscales

Millhead

Hagg
Wood

C

Wood
Tarn

Hunting Hill

Carnforth
Station

When you reach two gates on your right, take the second gate then turn almost immediately left through a gap in the wall and follow the path down to a small car park. Go through the car park and out onto the road, turning left to drop down into Warton Village. (*You can take a diversion right here to see the church and the rectory.*)

When you reach the village turn left and continue past the Washington house (on your right) until you reach Borwick Lane. Turn right along Borwick Lane then, just after Back Lane, right again into a driveway. Turn immediately left to follow the enclosed bridleway and remain on this until you pass the last house on the right. (**Point A**) (*To reach Senset Well continue straight on, along the enclosed path, until you reach the spring and small pond. To return to the route retrace your steps to* **Point A**.)

Follow the path along the back of the houses and continue through a kissing gate. Remain on the path alongside the field boundary, crossing into the next field, and follow the path as it leads around the field to a stone stile on the far side – cross this stile and continue on to a wooden stile. (NOTE do not cross the stile leading alongside the school grounds.) Cross the stile and follow the path as it bears right to emerge through an alley onto the road and turn left. (**Point B**)

[*Exit point for short walk: remain on the High Street, bear right into Sand Lane then turn right along the track after the last house to bring you to* **Point D**.]

Pass The Malt Shovel pub and turn left following a tarmac track crossing a children's play area. At the wall on the far side turn right along the narrow path and round into a cul-de-sac. Turn right and cross the road then turn left to follow the clearly signed public foot-path to Millhead. Pass through two metal kissing gates and remain on the clearly trodden and way marked route as it crosses open fields and eventually becomes hard track as it reaches Millhead.

When you emerge onto the road turn left towards the railway bridge then immediately right underneath the bridge to follow Shore Road (**Point C**). Remain on this road walking alongside the river until you reach a wooden footbridge. Cross the bridge and follow the tarmac track up to the road.

Turn right to cross the railway bridge then left at the T Junction. After 50 metres turn left and pass through two wide metal gates and turn right to follow a concrete track running alongside the road. Remain on this track until you reach the second metal gate on your right – pass through the gate and turn left along the road a short way to reach a stone stile crossing into a field on your right signposted to Warton. (*This may be overgrown so look carefully, it's on the right before the bend.*)

Cross the stile and bear slight right to cross the field up to another stile. Cross this and continue on with the field boundary on your immediate left, cross another stone stile and keep going until you reach a very narrow stone stile leading into the field on your left, cross this then turn hard right, alongside the buildings. Remain on this path with the field boundary on your right until the path is crossed by another path at the second field boundary (**Point D**) – turn left here and follow the path uphill towards Warton Crag.

At the top of the field pass through the stone stile and out onto the lane. Turn right to return to the nature reserve car park.

A tale about a town

Warton is such a beautifully quiet little village that it's hard to believe just how much has gone on here in the past. Its name derives from the old English 'tun' (town) by the 'weard' (look out) and indicates its strategic importance alongside Warton Crag.

As with much of the local area the limestone rocks played an important part, but so did farming with village streets such as Hemplands (just off the High Street), reminding us of the importance of wool in the town's history – the census of 1841 still recorded handloom weaving as an ongoing activity in the town.

At the start of the fourteenth century Warton was a bustling town but then began a run of bad luck. In 1316 and 1322 the Scottish armies of Robert the Bruce came through and laid waste to the area; this was followed by a severe famine and then the Black Death arrived in 1349, reducing Warton from a local focal point to a small rural village.

Field quarry

Today Warton sits near a number of important transportation routes – the M6, the A6 and the west coast mainline, and it was the same in the past, though the methods of transportation were a little different. The Coach Road is so named

because it was the route the mail coach took through the area, and the town was close to the important west coast route to Scotland. This section of the route forms part of the Morecambe Bay Cycleway which stretches 130 km (81 miles) from Walney Island in the north around to Glasson Dock in the south.

The area also played an important part in the birth of another major transportation route. Rock from the quarry at the start of the walk was used in the building of Britain's first motorway, the Preston

bypass, which opened in 1958 and now forms part of the M6 (from J29 at Bamber Bridge to J32 for the M55). The area in general has been quarried for limestone and associated metalliferous minerals since before Roman times.

Warton was also one of many starting points for routes across Morecambe Bay. Travel across the bay was as dangerous back then as it is today, but back then the roads on the land were, in many cases, worse. Where we now see miles of undulating tarmac there was once nothing more than boggy tracks, leaving travellers stuck between a rock and a hard place (or a bog and a sandy place). After the turnpike acts of the seventeenth and eighteenth centuries the roads in the area improved – with routes around the base of the crag preferable to those over it. Towards the end of the route as you cross the railway and walk on the concrete path alongside the road you're following one of the old toll roads and the toll house once stood on the grassy area on the bend in the road.

One of the most famous names connected with Warton is George Washington – first president of the United States. His ancestors lived in Warton in the fifteenth century and paid for the building of the

US flag at Warton Church

tower on the church. To commemorate this a stone was laid at the base of the tower with the Washington family crest on – three stars above two stripes, which went on to form the basis of the US flag. It's worth a short detour from the walk to take a look inside (the church is usually open). The old stone is now inside the base of the tower in the church kitchen directly above the kettle; it's a little weathered but you can still just about make out the crest. On 4 July each year the stars and stripes are flown from the church tower to commemorate the connection.

While you're in the village take a look at the rectory, which dates from the fourteenth century and gives a good indication of how rich and important the town once was. Although it fell out of use as a rectory by 1721, there was a cottage built at its north end which was occupied until the twentieth century.

Warton Rectory

Nearby Carnforth has also had a big impact on Warton and Millhead (originally named as it was the site of Warton's corn mills). During the late 1800s the railways and iron works proliferated in Carnforth at such a terrific rate that the owners were forced to scour the country in order to find sufficient labour to keep them running. At the same time iron production in the West Midlands had slumped badly so many workers relocated from there to Millhead – so many in fact that between 1860 and 1929 over 100 new houses were built to accommodate them and the town earned the nickname 'Dudley'.

Carnforth station (another short detour from the route) is also known to many of us as Milford Junction from *Brief Encounter*, as it was used as a location for the film. The infamous tea rooms in the film were actually built as a set in the film studios but they have now been lovingly recreated at the station and make for the perfect mid walk detour and stopping off point to enjoy cup of tea, a cake and visit to the *Brief Encounter* museum.

Warton star

Bibliography

Ayre, Barry, *From Keer to Kent: a Look at Life in the Arnside/Silverdale Area of Outstanding Natural Beauty*, (Barry Ayre: Carnforth, 2001)

Barnes, J. A., *All Around Arnside* (Titus Wilson: Kendal, 1933)

Bolton, T. E., Fogg, I. J., *Silverdale, its History, People and Places* (Howe: London, 1978)

Bradbury, Dennis, *Arnside A Guide and Community History* (Stramongate Press: Kendal, 2002)

Denwood, Andy, *Leighton Moss: Ice Age to Present Day* (Palatine Books: Lancaster, 2014)

Harper, Charles. S., *The Manchester and Glasgow Road* (Cecil Palmer: London, 1924)

Hutton, Rev. William, *The Beetham Repository, 1770* (Titus Wilson: Kendal, 1906)

Kelly's Directory of Cumberland and Westmorland 1938 (Kelly's Directories Ltd: London, 1934)

Lofthouse, J. *Lancashire & Westmorland Highways* (Robert Hale Ltd: London, 1953)

Mitchell, W. R., *All Around Morecambe Bay* (Phillimore & Co Ltd: Chichester, 2008)

Mourholme Local History Society, *How it Was, A North Lancashire Parish in the Seventeenth Century* (Mourholme Society: Carnforth, 1998)

Mourholme Local History Society, *Warton 1800–1850: How a North Lancashire Parish Changed* (Mourholme Society: Carnforth, 2005)

Palmer, W. T. *The Verge of Lakeland* (Robert Hale Ltd: London, 1933)

Peter, David, *In and Around Silverdale* (Barry Ayre: Carnforth, 1984)

Peter, David, *Warton with Lindeth, A History, Part 1* (Warton History Group and Lancashire County Council Library and Leisure Committee, 1985)

Rawlinson Ford, J., and Fuller-Maitland, J. A. (eds), *John Lucas's History of Warton Parish, 1710–1744*, (Titus Wilson: Kendal, 1931)

Royal Commission on Historical Monuments, an inventory of Westmorland 1936 (HMSO: London, 1936)

McIntire, W. T. (ed.), *Transactions of the Cumberland and Westmorland Antiquarian and Archaeological Society*, Volume XXXVII (Titus Wilson: Kendal, 1937)

Waugh, Edwin, *In the Lake Country* (John Heywood: Manchester, 1880)

Williams, Simon., *The Matchless Tragedy* (Mourholme Local History Society; Carnforth, 2013)

Websites:

http://www.british-history.ac.uk
http://www.wildlifetrusts.org
https://www.rspb.org.uk
http://www.arnsidesilverdaleaonb.org.uk
http://www.mourholme.co.uk
http://www.morecambebay.org.uk
http://arnsidevillage.co.uk